Better Homes and Gardens®

POULTRY RECIPES

Our seal assures you that every recipe in *Poultry Recipes*
has been tested in the Better Homes and Gardens® Test Kitchen.
This means that each recipe is practical and reliable,
and meets our high standards of taste appeal.

For years, Better Homes and Gardens® Books has been a leader in publishing cook books. In *Poultry Recipes,* we've pulled together a delicious collection of recipes from several of our latest best-sellers. These no-fail recipes will make your cooking easier and more enjoyable.

Editor: Rosemary C. Hutchinson
Editorial Project Manager: Rosanne Weber Mattson
Graphic Designer: Harijs Priekulis
Electronic Text Processor: Paula Forest

On the front cover: Orange Chicken *(see recipe, page 22)*

Contents

Apple-Pecan Chicken

1 cup pecan halves	● Place pecans in a shallow baking dish. Bake in a 350° oven for 8 to 10 minutes or till toasted.
2 whole large skinned and boned chicken breasts, halved lengthwise **⅓ cup cranberry *or* cranberry-apple juice cocktail** **1 tablespoon brown sugar** **1½ teaspoons cornstarch** **⅛ teaspoon ground nutmeg** **⅛ teaspoon ground cinnamon**	● Meanwhile, cut chicken into 1-inch pieces. For sauce, in a small mixing bowl stir together cranberry or cranberry-apple juice cocktail, brown sugar, cornstarch, nutmeg, and cinnamon. Set aside.
1 tablespoon cooking oil **⅔ cup cranberries**	● Preheat a wok or large skillet over high heat. Add cooking oil. Add *half* of the chicken to wok or skillet. Stir-fry for 2 to 3 minutes or till no longer pink. Remove chicken. Repeat with remaining chicken. Return all chicken to wok or skillet. Stir in cranberries. Push mixture to sides.
1 large green apple, sliced	● Stir sauce. Add to center of wok or skillet. Cook and stir till thickened and bubbly. Cook and stir for 30 seconds more. Stir in apple slices. Cook, covered, for 2 minutes. Stir in the toasted pecan halves. Serve immediately. Serves 4.

Pecans are genuine, wholesome, grown-in-America originals. Early colonists were introduced to the native nut by the Indians, and it has become an important part of our cuisine.

Orange Turkey Tenderloins

1 teaspoon finely shredded
   orange peel
½ cup orange juice
¼ cup water
2 tablespoons dry sherry
2 teaspoons cornstarch
1½ teaspoons instant chicken
   bouillon granules

● For sauce, in a small mixing bowl stir together orange peel, orange juice, water, sherry, cornstarch, and chicken bouillon granules. Set aside.

Let's talk turkey. Fresh turkey breast tenderloins are very lean cuts of white meat that are skinless and boneless. You can expect to find two to four pieces in a one-pound package.

4 fresh turkey breast
   tenderloins (about 1½
   pounds total)
2 tablespoons cooking oil
3 medium carrots, thinly
   sliced

● In a large skillet cook turkey in hot oil for 4 to 5 minutes on each side or till tender. Remove from skillet. Reduce heat to medium. Add carrots to skillet. Cook and stir for 6 to 8 minutes or till tender.
   Push carrots to side of skillet. Stir sauce. Add sauce to skillet. Cook and stir till thickened and bubbly. Return turkey to skillet. Cover and cook about 2 minutes more or till turkey is heated through. Makes 4 servings.

Microwave directions: For sauce, in a 2-cup glass measure stir together orange peel, orange juice, *2 tablespoons* water, sherry, cornstarch, and chicken bouillon granules. Set aside.
   In a 12x7½x2-inch microwave-safe baking dish combine turkey, carrots, and 2 tablespoons *water*. (Omit oil.) Micro-cook, covered, on 100% power (high) for 7 to 8 minutes or till turkey and carrots are tender, rearranging turkey pieces after 4 minutes. Drain and set aside.
   Stir sauce. Cook, uncovered, on high for 2 to 4 minutes or till thickened and bubbly, stirring every minute. Serve over turkey and carrots.

Ginger-Walnut Chicken

1 whole large skinned and boned chicken breast, halved lengthwise Salt Pepper	● Place 1 piece of chicken between 2 pieces of clear plastic wrap. Pound to ¼-inch thickness. Repeat with remaining chicken. Sprinkle with salt and pepper.	
1 tablespoon butter *or* margarine	● Meanwhile, in a large skillet melt butter or margarine. Brown chicken in hot butter for 4 to 6 minutes or till tender, turning once. Remove from skillet. Keep chicken warm.	
2 teaspoons sugar 1 teaspoon cornstarch ½ cup orange juice 1 teaspoon grated gingerroot 2 tablespoons coarsely chopped walnuts*	● Stir together sugar and cornstarch. Stir in orange juice and gingerroot. Add to skillet. Cook and stir till thickened and bubbly. Cook and stir 2 minutes more. Add chicken, turning to coat. Sprinkle with nuts. Makes 2 servings.	**If you don't have time to toast the walnuts, don't worry about it. Just use the untoasted ones. You'll still get a nice nutty flavor.**

*Note: If desired, toast the walnuts by placing them in a single layer on a baking sheet. Bake in a 350° oven for 10 to 15 minutes or till the nuts are toasted.

Or, place 1 cup walnuts in a 2-cup glass measure. Micro-cook, uncovered, on 100% power (high) for 3 minutes, stirring every minute. Cook on high for 1 to 2 minutes more, stirring every 30 seconds. Let stand 15 minutes. The nuts will continue to toast while standing.

Pecan Hollandaise-Sauced Turkey

1 11-ounce package frozen long grain and wild rice
1 10-ounce package frozen asparagus spears
4 turkey breast slices (about ¾ pound)

● Prepare rice according to package directions. Meanwhile, cook asparagus in a small amount of boiling water for 5 to 7 minutes or till crisp-tender. Drain. Put ¼ of the asparagus spears crosswise onto *each* turkey slice. Roll up slices.

1 tablespoon butter *or* margarine, melted
⅛ teaspoon garlic salt

● Place turkey rolls, seam side down, in a greased 8x8x2-inch baking dish. Mix butter and garlic salt. Brush over turkey rolls. Bake in a 375° oven for 13 to 15 minutes or till turkey is no longer pink. Keep warm.

¼ cup pecan pieces
1 1-ounce envelope hollandaise sauce mix
Pecan halves (optional)

● Meanwhile, for pecan hollandaise, place pecans in a blender container. Cover. Blend till nuts are finely ground. Prepare hollandaise sauce mix according to package directions. Stir in ground pecans. Serve immediately over turkey rolls and rice. Top with pecan halves, if desired. Makes 4 servings.

Microwave directions: Prepare rice according to package directions. In an 8x8x2-inch microwave-safe baking dish combine asparagus and 2 tablespoons *water*. Micro-cook, covered with vented plastic wrap, on 100% power (high) for 4 to 6 minutes or just till asparagus is tender, stirring once. Drain.

Assemble turkey rolls as above. In a 6-ounce custard cup combine butter and garlic salt. Cook, uncovered, for 30 to 60 seconds or till butter is melted. Brush over turkey rolls. Cook, covered with vented plastic wrap, on high for 4 to 6 minutes or till turkey is no longer pink, rearranging turkey rolls and giving the dish a half-turn once. Keep warm.

Prepare pecan hollandaise as above. Serve as above.

Dine in instead of out tonight. It will give you the chance to savor the delicate blend of flavors of this gourmet fare, and you won't even have to leave a tip!

Creole Chicken

⅔ cup long grain rice
1 small onion, finely chopped (¼ cup)
¼ cup finely chopped green pepper
2 tablespoons butter *or* margarine
1 8-ounce can tomato sauce
1 4-ounce can mushroom stems and pieces, drained
½ teaspoon sugar
¼ to ½ teaspoon bottled hot pepper sauce
1 bay leaf

● Cook rice according to package directions. Meanwhile, in a large skillet cook onion and green pepper in butter or margarine till vegetables are tender but not brown. Stir in tomato sauce, mushrooms, sugar, hot pepper sauce, and bay leaf. Bring to boiling. Reduce the heat. Cook, uncovered, over medium-low heat for 5 minutes. Remove bay leaf.

Bring some of the charm of the Deep South to your table whenever you serve this spicy one-dish meal. It's inspired by the melting-pot cooking of old New Orleans.

2 whole large skinned and boned chicken breasts, halved lengthwise

● Meanwhile, place *each* chicken breast half, boned side up, between 2 pieces of clear plastic wrap. Working from the center to the edges, pound the chicken lightly with the fine-toothed or flat side of a meat mallet to ¼-inch thickness (see photo, below). Remove the plastic wrap. Place chicken pieces in the skillet. Spoon sauce over pieces. Cook, covered, over medium heat for 5 to 7 minutes or till meat is no longer pink. Serve over rice. Makes 4 servings.

Place the chicken piece between two pieces of clear plastic wrap and use the fine-toothed or flat side of a meat mallet to lightly pound the meat to the desired thickness.

Turkey Stroganoff

2 cups wide noodles (4 ounces)	● Cook noodles according to package directions. Drain. Set aside.
1 pound ground raw turkey 8 ounces fresh mushrooms, sliced (3 cups) 1 medium onion, chopped 1 teaspoon instant chicken bouillon granules ½ teaspoon dried thyme, crushed ½ teaspoon garlic salt ⅛ teaspoon ground nutmeg	● Meanwhile, in a 12-inch skillet cook ground turkey, mushrooms, and onion over medium heat till turkey is no longer pink and onion is tender but not brown, stirring occasionally to break up turkey. Stir in ¾ cup *water,* bouillon granules, thyme, garlic salt, and nutmeg.
3 tablespoons all-purpose flour 1 8-ounce carton dairy sour cream *or* plain yogurt Paprika (optional)	● In a small mixing bowl stir flour into sour cream or yogurt till smooth. Stir into skillet. Cook and stir over medium heat till thickened and bubbly. Cook for 1 minute more. Serve over noodles. Sprinkle with paprika, if desired. Makes 4 servings.

Sauces cooked in the microwave don't evaporate the same way they do on the range top. So, you'll need to cut the water a little when you make this recipe in the microwave oven.

Microwave directions: Cook noodles as above. In a 2-quart microwave-safe casserole, crumble the ground turkey. Micro-cook turkey, mushrooms, and onion, uncovered, on 100% power (high) for 7 to 10 minutes or till turkey is no longer pink and vegetables are tender, stirring twice. Stir in ⅔ *cup* water, bouillon granules, thyme, garlic salt, and nutmeg. In a small bowl stir the flour into the sour cream till smooth. Stir into turkey mixture. Cook, uncovered, on high for 7 to 10 minutes or till thickened and bubbly, stirring every 2 minutes. Cook for 30 seconds more. Serve as above.

Chicken Shortcakes

1 cup frozen peas and carrots 1 11-ounce can condensed cheddar cheese soup ¼ cup milk Several dashes bottled hot pepper sauce 1½ cups cubed cooked chicken	● In a medium saucepan cook the vegetables, covered, in ¼ cup *boiling water* for 5 minutes. Drain. In the same saucepan stir together soup, milk, and hot pepper sauce. Add chicken and cooked vegetables. Cook over medium heat about 10 minutes or till heated through, stirring occasionally.
6 rusks *or* 3 English muffins, split and toasted	● To serve, place *2* rusks or toasted English muffin halves on *each* of 3 dinner plates. Spoon chicken mixture over rusks or muffin halves. Serves 3.

We could have called this jiffy-quick chicken dish "Chicken Shortcuts" since it's only 20 minutes from start to finish. By either name, it tastes great—a surefire hit with kids, too.

Out of Your Hat

When drop-in guests stay for dinner, dazzle them with some menu magic. The secret to your wizardry—a cache of off-the-shelf ingredients that you transform into a spectacular meal for six (*see recipes, pages 14–15*).

Pictured, left to right:
Chicken and Pasta Voilà
Presto-Chango Antipasto
Grand Finale Torte
(*see recipes, pages 14–15*)

Out of Your Hat

MENU

Chicken and Pasta Voilà

Presto-Chango Antipasto

Hard rolls and butter

Grand Finale Torte

White wine or coffee

MENU COUNTDOWN

45 Minutes Ahead:
Place cans and jars of ingredients for Presto-Chango Antipasto in the freezer. Cook asparagus for antipasto. Chill. Prepare Grand Finale Torte. Chill.

30 Minutes Ahead:
Prepare Chicken and Pasta Voilà. Keep warm.

15 Minutes Ahead:
Make coffee. Arrange antipasto tray. Chill till serving time.

Presto-Chango Antipasto

Pictured on pages 12–13.

1 **8-ounce can sliced beets**	
1 **6-ounce jar marinated artichoke hearts**	
1 **3-ounce jar almond-stuffed olives**	
¾ **cup pickled peppers**	

● Chill unopened cans and jars of beets, artichoke hearts, olives, and peppers in the freezer for 30 minutes.

1 **10-ounce package frozen asparagus spears**

● Meanwhile, cook asparagus spears according to package directions. Drain. Rinse with cold water. Drain well. Chill in the refrigerator for at least 15 minutes or till serving time.
  Drain beets, artichoke hearts, and olives. Arrange all ingredients on a platter. Chill till serving time. Serves 6.

Pick a peck of pickled peppers in the pickle section of your supermarket. Good choices for your antipasto tray are pepper-oncini, pickled cherry peppers, pickled jalapeño chili peppers, or pickled yellow chili peppers.

Chicken and Pasta Voilà

Pictured on pages 12–13.

8 ounces linguine *or* spaghetti, broken 1 10-ounce package frozen cut broccoli	● Cook pasta in a large amount of boiling salted water for 5 minutes. Add broccoli. Return to boiling. Cook for 4 to 5 minutes more or till broccoli is crisp-tender. Drain.
1 10¾-ounce can condensed chicken broth ½ cup dry white wine 1 tablespoon dried minced onion 1 teaspoon Italian seasoning ½ teaspoon dried minced garlic *or* garlic powder ½ teaspoon white pepper 1 tablespoon cornstarch 1 tablespoon cold water	● Meanwhile, in a 10-inch skillet stir together chicken broth, wine, onion, Italian seasoning, garlic, and pepper. Bring to boiling. Reduce heat. Cover and simmer for 5 minutes. In a small bowl combine cornstarch and water. Stir into broth mixture. Cook and stir till thickened and bubbly.
3 cups chopped cooked chicken 2 tablespoons diced pimiento Parmesan cheese	● Stir chicken and pimiento into broth mixture. Cook and stir about 2 minutes or till heated through. In a large bowl toss broth mixture with pasta and broccoli till coated. Pass Parmesan cheese. Makes 6 servings.

The pepper goes under-cover in this delicious sauce. You may not see the white pepper, but you'll taste it.

White pepper and black pepper come from the same vine. For black pepper, the grains—not yet ripe when picked—are dried with the outer peel, which turns black. For white pepper, the berries, ripe when picked, are peeled before drying.

Grand Finale Torte

Pictured on pages 12–13.

1 frozen loaf pound cake ½ teaspoon finely shredded lemon peel ½ cup strawberry preserves	● Cut frozen pound cake horizontally into 3 layers. In a small bowl stir lemon peel into preserves. Spread *half* of the preserves mixture over bottom layer of cake. Top with second layer. Spread with remaining preserves. Top with third layer.
⅓ cup semisweet chocolate pieces 2 teaspoons shortening Slivered almonds (optional)	● In a small saucepan melt together chocolate pieces and shortening. Using a spoon, drizzle the chocolate mixture over top layer of cake. If desired, garnish with almonds. Chill in the refrigerator till serving time. Makes 6 servings.

The drizzle of chocolate makes this easy torte a brilliant conclusion to your show.

PDQ-BBQ Turkey

½ cup catsup 2 tablespoons brown sugar 2 tablespoons water 1 tablespoon vinegar 1 teaspoon Worcestershire sauce ¼ teaspoon crushed red pepper ¼ teaspoon ground cinnamon	● For sauce, in a 2-cup glass measure stir together catsup, brown sugar, water, vinegar, Worcestershire sauce, red pepper, and cinnamon. Micro-cook, uncovered, on 100% power (high) for 1½ to 2½ minutes or till bubbly, stirring once. Set mixture aside.
2 turkey drumsticks (about 1 pound each) *or* 2 to 2½ pounds meaty chicken pieces (breasts, wings, thighs, and drumsticks)	● In a 12x7½x2-inch microwave-safe baking dish arrange turkey or chicken pieces, skin side down, with meatiest portions toward the outside. Cook, loosely covered with waxed paper, on high for 8 minutes, giving dish a half-turn once. (Note: If using turkey, shield ends of drumsticks with foil, provided the owner's manual permits the use of metal in your particular microwave oven.) Drain well.
	● Brush turkey or chicken with sauce. Turn and brush again. Cook, covered loosely with waxed paper, on high for 6 to 8 minutes more or till turkey is no longer pink (allow 4 to 6 minutes for chicken). Remove baking dish from microwave. Keep warm. Cook remaining sauce, uncovered, on high for 1 to 2 minutes or till hot. Pass with turkey or chicken. Makes 4 servings.
	Micro-Plus Grilled Chicken: Prepare chicken as above, *except* after cooking for 8 minutes, transfer to a preheated grill. Arrange chicken, skin side down, directly over *medium* coals. Brush with sauce. Grill for 5 minutes. Turn. Brush with sauce. Grill for 6 to 8 minutes more or till done, brushing often with sauce.

Microwave Manicotti

4	**manicotti shells**
1	**tablespoon cooking oil**
1	**beaten egg**
½	**cup ricotta *or* cream-style cottage cheese, drained**
½	**cup shredded mozzarella cheese (2 ounces)**
2	**tablespoons grated Parmesan cheese**

● In a 1½-quart microwave-safe casserole combine manicotti shells, oil, and 3 cups *hottest tap water*. Micro-cook, uncovered, on 100% power (high) for 12 to 14 minutes or till almost done, rearranging shells twice. Cover dish and set aside.

Meanwhile, in a small bowl combine the egg, ricotta or cottage cheese, mozzarella cheese, Parmesan cheese, and ¼ teaspoon *pepper*. Set aside.

The trick to manicotti in 40 minutes is making the most of your microwave. In this recipe, cooking the manicotti in just 3 cups of water saves you the time of boiling a big pot of water on the range top.

½	**pound ground raw turkey**
1	**cup meatless spaghetti sauce with mushrooms**
½	**teaspoon dried minced onion**
¼	**teaspoon Italian seasoning, crushed**
	Snipped parsley (optional)

● In a 1-quart microwave-safe casserole crumble ground turkey. Cook, covered, on high for 2 to 3 minutes or till turkey is no longer pink, stirring twice. Drain. Stir in spaghetti sauce, dried onion, and Italian seasoning. Drain manicotti shells and rinse under cold water.

Stuff ¼ of the cheese mixture into *each* shell. Pour *half* of the meat mixture into a 10x6x2-inch microwave-safe baking dish. Place shells atop. Spread remaining sauce over shells. Cook, covered with vented plastic wrap, on high for 4 to 5 minutes or till heated through, giving dish a half-turn once. Garnish with parsley, if desired. Serves 2.

Turkey and Carrot Patties

1 small carrot, shredded (¼ cup) 2 tablespoons water ½ teaspoon minced dried onion	● In a mixing bowl stir together shredded carrot, water, and minced dried onion. Cover with vented clear plastic wrap. Micro-cook on 100% power (high) about 1½ minutes or till the shredded carrot is tender. Drain.
1 beaten egg 2 tablespoons fine dry bread crumbs ¼ teaspoon salt ¼ teaspoon poultry seasoning ½ pound ground raw turkey	● Stir beaten egg, fine dry bread crumbs, salt, and poultry seasoning into the carrot mixture. Add ground raw turkey; mix well. Shape the meat mixture into two ½-inch-thick patties. (Mixture will be soft.)
	● Place patties in a shallow baking dish. Cover with vented clear plastic wrap. Cook on high for 4 to 5 minutes or till no pink remains, rotating the dish a half-turn every 2 minutes. Let stand, covered, for 1 minute. Makes 2 servings.

Try ground turkey as an alternative to ground beef. It's lower in calories and fat than most other ground meats.

Quick-as-a-Wink Chicken à la King

1   10¾-ounce can condensed cream of mushroom soup
⅓   cup milk
2   tablespoons dry sherry
¼   teaspoon pepper
2   cups diced cooked chicken
1½ cups frozen peas
2   tablespoons sliced pimiento, chopped (optional)
    Toast points

● In a 1½-quart microwave-safe casserole stir together cream of mushroom soup, milk, sherry, and pepper. Stir in chicken, peas, and, if desired, pimiento. Micro-cook, covered, on 100% power (high) for 7 to 8 minutes or till mixture is heated through, stirring twice. Serve over toast points. Makes 4 servings.

Cooked poultry doesn't keep long. After a big chicken dinner, plan to use any leftovers within two days. If that's a problem, freeze the chicken in moisture- and vaporproof wrap. That way, you can keep it for about a month.

Cock-a-Noodle Casserole

3   ounces medium noodles (1½ cups)
½   cup frozen mixed vegetables
1   10¾-ounce can condensed cream of chicken soup
1   4-ounce package (1 cup) shredded cheddar cheese
½   cup milk
½   cup dairy sour cream

● Prepare noodles according to package directions. Drain. Meanwhile, place vegetables in a colander. Run under cold water till thawed. Drain and set aside.
    In a 2-quart microwave-safe casserole combine soup, *half* of the cheese, milk, and sour cream.

1   5-ounce can chunk-style chicken, drained and flaked

● Stir cooked noodles, thawed vegetables, and chicken into soup mixture. Micro-cook, covered, on 100% power (high) for 8 to 10 minutes or till mixture is heated through, stirring once.

¼   cup toasted wheat germ

● Sprinkle remaining cheese on top. Sprinkle with wheat germ. Cook, uncovered, on high for 1 to 2 minutes more or till cheese melts. Makes 4 servings.

Make the most of available convenience products to shortcut recipes. In Cock-a-Noodle Casserole, you skip a step by buying cheese that's already shredded. Look for more work-saving ingredients—such as chopped nuts, frozen chopped onion, frozen chopped green pepper, minced dried onion, and minced dried garlic—to help shortcut other recipes in this book.

Chicken Cacciatore

4 ounces tiny shell *or* cork-screw macaroni (1⅓ cups)	● Cook the macaroni according to the package directions. Let stand, covered.
1 8-ounce can tomato sauce **½ teaspoon sugar** **¼ teaspoon dried basil, crushed** **¼ teaspoon dried marjoram, crushed**	● For sauce, in a mixing bowl stir together tomato sauce, sugar, dried basil, and dried marjoram.
2 whole medium skinned and boned chicken breasts, halved lengthwise	● Arrange the chicken breast halves in a 10x6x2-inch microwave-safe baking dish. Pour the tomato sauce mixture over the chicken. Cover with waxed paper. Micro-cook on 100% power (high) for 6 to 8½ minutes or till chicken is no longer pink.
1 1½-ounce slice mozzarella cheese **Snipped parsley**	● Cut cheese slice into 4 equal pieces. Lay *one* piece of cheese on top of *each* chicken breast half. Cook, uncovered, on high about 1 minute or till cheese melts. 　Drain the macaroni. Arrange the chicken and sauce atop the macaroni. Sprinkle with the parsley. Makes 4 servings.

Cacciatore (pronounced kotch-a-TOR-e) is an Italian word that means cooked with tomatoes and herbs. This chicken dish has not only tomato sauce and herbs, but also cheese and pasta.

Rub-a-Dub Tub Chicken

2 cups crisp rice cereal, crushed ¼ cup toasted wheat germ ½ teaspoon Italian seasoning ½ teaspoon paprika	● In a mixing bowl, stir together the crushed cereal, wheat germ, Italian seasoning, paprika, and ¼ teaspoon *salt*.	**This seasoned coated chicken gets a hint of Italy from the Italian seasoning.**
2 tablespoons butter *or* margarine	● Micro-cook the butter or margarine on 100% power (high) for 15 to 45 seconds or till melted.	
1 2½- to 3-pound broiler-fryer chicken, cut up	● Rinse chicken and pat dry with a paper towel. Brush chicken with melted butter. Coat with cereal mixture.	
	● Place a microwave-safe rack or 2 microwave-safe upside-down saucers in a 12x7½x2-inch microwave-safe baking dish. Arrange chicken on top, with the meatiest parts toward the outside. Sprinkle any remaining cereal mixture on top. Cover with waxed paper. Cook on high for 12 to 16 minutes or till no longer pink, turning the dish once. Makes 6 servings.	

Chic'n-Lic'n Nuggets

2 whole medium skinned and boned chicken breasts, halved lengthwise 1 tablespoon water	● In a 9-inch microwave-safe pie plate combine chicken and 1 tablespoon water. Cover with waxed paper. Micro-cook on 100% power (high) for 5 to 6 minutes or till chicken is no longer pink, turning the dish once. Let stand 5 minutes.	**Eat these juicy chunks of chicken with your fingers or a fork, or spear them with toothpicks. Choose from three sauces— barbecue, sweet-sour, or mustard-mayonnaise. Heat the sauce in the microwave oven and dip the nuggets in.**
1 slightly beaten egg 1 tablespoon water 16 rich round crackers	● In a mixing bowl combine egg and water. In a plastic bag, crush the crackers. When chicken is cool enough to handle, cut chicken into bite-size chunks. Dip chunks into egg mixture, then roll in crushed crackers.	
2 tablespoons butter *or* margarine	● In a microwave-safe pie plate cook the butter or margarine, uncovered, for 15 to 45 seconds or till melted. Add chicken. Cook, uncovered, for 1 minute. Use a wooden spoon to stir. Cook, uncovered, for 1 to 2 minutes more or till hot.	
½ cup bottled barbecue sauce, sweet-sour sauce, *or* mustard-mayonnaise sandwich and salad sauce	● Put sauce into a small microwave-safe bowl. Cook, uncovered, about 1 minute or till hot. To serve, dip the chicken into sauce. Makes 4 servings.	

Orange Chicken

Pictured on the cover.

4 **chicken drumsticks and 4 chicken thighs, skinned and frozen (2 pounds total)** 2 **small green *or* sweet red peppers, cut into strips**	● In a 3½-, 4-, 5-, or 6-quart crockery cooker, place *frozen* chicken. Top with green or red pepper.
½ **cup chicken broth** ½ **cup orange juice** ½ **cup catsup** 2 **tablespoons soy sauce** 1 **tablespoon molasses** 1 **teaspoon dry mustard** ½ **teaspoon garlic salt** ⅛ **teaspoon pepper**	● In a bowl stir together broth, orange juice, catsup, soy sauce, molasses, dry mustard, garlic salt, and pepper.
	● Pour broth mixture over chicken. Cover; cook on low-heat setting for 10 to 12 hours or high-heat setting for 4½ to 6½ hours. Transfer chicken and peppers to a serving platter. Cover to keep warm. Reserve drippings.
1 **11-ounce can mandarin orange sections** 2 **teaspoons cornstarch**	● For sauce, skim fat from drippings. Measure *1 cup* cooking liquid. Transfer to a saucepan. Drain oranges, reserving *1 tablespoon juice.* Stir together reserved juice and cornstarch. Add to liquid in the saucepan. Cook and stir till thickened and bubbly. Cook and stir for 2 minutes more. Stir in oranges. Heat through.
Hot cooked rice	● Serve sauce and chicken mixture over rice. Makes 4 servings.

You also can wait till after work and prepare this dish in the oven. Simply follow the recipe as directed, *except* arrange the crockery cooker ingredients in a 2- or 3-quart casserole. Cover and bake in a 350° oven about 1 hour or till no pink remains.

Turkey Roast Chablis

¾ **cup dry white wine** ½ **cup chopped onion** 1 **clove garlic, minced** 1 **bay leaf**	● In a 3½-, 4-, 5-, or 6-quart crockery cooker combine white wine, onion, garlic, and bay leaf.
1 **3- to 3½-pound frozen boneless turkey roast, thawed** 1 **teaspoon dried rosemary, crushed** ¼ **teaspoon pepper**	● If turkey roast is wrapped in netting, remove netting and discard. If gravy packet is present, remove packet from roast; refrigerate packet for another use. Combine rosemary and pepper. Rub roast with rosemary mixture. Place turkey roast in cooker. Cover; cook on low-heat setting for 10 to 12 hours or on high-heat setting for 4½ to 5½ hours. Remove roast and keep warm.
⅓ **cup light cream or milk** 2 **tablespoons cornstarch** ⅛ **teaspoon salt**	● For gravy, strain cooking juices; discard solids. Skim fat from juices. Measure 1⅓ cups juices into a small saucepan. Combine cream or milk, cornstarch, and salt; stir into juices. Cook and stir till thickened and bubbly. Cook and stir for 2 minutes more.
	● Slice turkey roast. Spoon some gravy over roast. Pass remaining gravy with roast. Makes 6 to 8 servings.

White wine and rosemary give a mild seasoning to the gravy.

Barbecue-Style Turkey Thighs

½ **cup catsup** 2 **tablespoons brown sugar** 1 **tablespoon quick-cooking tapioca** 1 **tablespoon vinegar** 1 **teaspoon Worcestershire sauce** ¼ **teaspoon ground cinnamon** ¼ **teaspoon crushed red pepper**	● In a 3½- or 4-quart crockery cooker combine catsup, brown sugar, tapioca, vinegar, Worcestershire sauce, cinnamon, and red pepper.
2 **to 2½ pounds turkey thighs (about 2 thighs) or meaty chicken pieces (breasts, thighs, and drumsticks), skinned and frozen** **Hot cooked rice or noodles (optional)**	● Place *frozen* turkey thighs or chicken pieces atop catsup mixture, meaty side down and flat in the cooker. Cover; cook on low-heat setting for 10 to 12 hours or high-heat setting for 5 to 6 hours. Serve turkey or chicken and sauce over rice or noodles, if desired. Makes 4 to 6 servings.

Trim the turkey thighs, if necessary, before freezing them so they'll lie flat in the cooker. That way, they'll cook more evenly and have a richer barbecue flavor.

Tarragon Chicken with Squash and Apple Rings

1 medium acorn squash
(about 1 pound)
2 large cooking apples, cored
2 whole medium chicken breasts, halved lengthwise
Salt
Pepper

● Cut squash crosswise into 1-inch-thick rings. Discard seeds. Slice each apple into 4 rings.

In a 13x9x2-inch baking dish arrange chicken breasts in a row down half of the dish. Alternate and overlap squash and apple rings down the other half of the dish (see photo, below). Sprinkle lightly with salt and pepper.

The apple of your eye for this dish should be Rome Beauty, York Imperial, Newtown Pippin, Gravenstein, Granny Smith, or Golden Delicious.

¼ cup butter or margarine, melted
2 tablespoons lemon juice
1½ teaspoons dried tarragon, crushed
1 teaspoon paprika

● Stir together butter or margarine, lemon juice, tarragon, and paprika. Brush over chicken, squash, and apples. Cover and bake in a 350° oven about 50 minutes or till chicken is done and squash and apples are tender. Transfer to a serving platter with a slotted spoon. Makes 4 servings.

Arrange the chicken breasts in a lengthwise row down half of the baking dish. Alternate and overlap the squash and apple rings down the other half of the dish. Red cooking apples are particularly attractive with the squash.

Chicken Enchiladas

¼ cup chopped pecans ¼ cup chopped onion 2 tablespoons butter *or* margarine	● In a skillet cook ¼ cup pecans and onion in butter or margarine till onion is tender and pecans are lightly toasted. Remove from heat.	**These nut-topped enchiladas are so rich and creamy that one of them makes an ample helping. Serve with a refreshing green or fruit salad and your favorite rice dish. Though the enchiladas are fairly mild, you may want to have a cold beverage handy to put out an occasional jalapeño fire.**
1 3-ounce package cream cheese, softened 1 tablespoon milk ½ teaspoon salt ¼ teaspoon ground cumin 2 cups chopped cooked chicken	● In a bowl combine softened cream cheese, 1 tablespoon milk, salt, and ground cumin. Add nut mixture and chopped cooked chicken. Stir together till well combined.	
6 8-inch flour tortillas	● Spoon about *⅓ cup* chicken mixture onto *each* tortilla near one edge; roll up. Place filled tortillas, seam side down, in a greased 12x7½x2-inch baking dish.	
1 10¾-ounce can condensed cream of chicken soup 1 8-ounce carton dairy sour cream 1 cup milk 5 *or* 6 pickled jalapeño peppers, rinsed, seeded, and chopped (⅓ cup)	● In a bowl combine cream of chicken soup, sour cream, 1 cup milk, and the chopped pickled jalapeño peppers. Pour the soup mixture evenly over the tortillas in the baking dish. Cover with foil; bake in a 350° oven about 35 minutes or till heated through.	
1 cup shredded Monterey Jack *or* cheddar cheese (4 ounces) 2 tablespoons chopped pecans	● Remove foil. Sprinkle enchiladas with cheese and 2 tablespoons pecans. Return to the 350° oven for 4 to 5 minutes or till cheese is melted. Makes 6 servings.	

2 Spread 2 tablespoons of filling in the center of each chicken breast.

1 Stir the ingredients together in a small bowl.

Chicken Bundles

1 2½-ounce jar sliced mushrooms, drained
¼ cup shredded mozzarella *or* Monterey Jack cheese (1 ounce)
¼ cup plain yogurt
1 tablespoon chopped pimiento
2 teaspoons dried parsley flakes
4 boned skinless chicken breast halves (about 1 pound)

● In a mixing bowl stir together drained mushrooms, cheese, yogurt, pimiento, and parsley flakes. Spread *2 rounded tablespoons* of mixture on each piece of chicken. Fold chicken over filling. Fasten with wooden toothpicks.

1 tablespoon butter *or* margarine
Grated Parmesan cheese

● Place chicken bundles, toothpick side up, in a 10x6x2-inch baking dish. In a small saucepan melt butter or margarine. Brush tops with melted butter. Sprinkle with Parmesan cheese. Bake chicken bundles in a 350° oven for 40 to 45 minutes or till chicken is no longer pink. Makes 4 servings.

3 After brushing the tops of the chicken breasts with margarine, sprinkle with Parmesan cheese.

Lazy-Day Chicken Lasagna

1 cup spaghetti sauce with mushrooms 1 cup cut-up cooked chicken ½ teaspoon dried basil, crushed	● In a mixing bowl combine spaghetti sauce with mushrooms, cooked chicken, and dried basil. Set the spaghetti sauce-chicken mixture aside.

The timesaving trick here is to assemble the lasagna using uncooked noodles.

1 beaten egg ¾ cup cream-style cottage cheese, drained ¼ cup grated Parmesan cheese 1 tablespoon dried parsley flakes ⅛ teaspoon pepper	● In a mixing bowl stir together the beaten egg, cream-style cottage cheese, grated Parmesan cheese, dried parsley flakes, and pepper.

4 lasagna noodles 1 cup shredded mozzarella cheese (4 ounces)	● Place 2 of the *uncooked* lasagna noodles in a 10x6x2-inch baking dish. Layer with *half* of the chicken mixture, *half* of the cottage cheese mixture, and *half* of the shredded mozzarella cheese. Repeat the layers, *except* for the remaining mozzarella cheese.

To test the noodles for doneness, prick them with a fork.

⅓ cup boiling water	● Pour boiling water into the dish around the edges. Cover tightly with foil. Bake in a 350° oven about 60 minutes or till lasagna noodles are tender. Sprinkle with the remaining shredded mozzarella cheese. Let stand, covered, for 10 minutes. Makes 4 servings.

Chicken with Pecan-Rice Stuffing

Make stuffing easier by placing the bird, neck side down, in a mixing bowl. Lightly spoon the rice mixture into the body cavity of the bird.

¾ cup chopped onion
¾ cup chopped celery
¼ cup snipped parsley
¼ cup butter *or* margarine
2 cups cooked rice
½ cup chopped pecans
½ teaspoon salt
¼ teaspoon dried marjoram,
    crushed
¼ teaspoon dried thyme,
    crushed
¼ teaspoon pepper
	● For stuffing, in a medium saucepan cook the chopped onion, chopped celery, and snipped parsley in butter or margarine till onion and celery are tender but not brown.
	
	    Remove from heat. Stir in the cooked rice, chopped pecans, the ½ teaspoon salt, marjoram, thyme, and pepper.

1 4- to 5-pound whole
    roasting chicken *or* one
    6- to 7-pound capon
  Salt
	● Rinse the roasting chicken or capon; pat excess moisture from the bird with paper towels. Sprinkle inside of cavities with the additional salt.
	
	    Spoon some of the stuffing mixture into the neck cavity. Skewer neck skin to back of bird. Lightly spoon the stuffing into body cavity; *do not* pack. Tie legs to tail with cord and twist wing tips under back, as shown at right.

	● Place any remaining stuffing in center of a piece of *heavy* foil; bring up long edges of foil and, leaving a little space for expansion of steam, seal tightly with a double fold. Then fold short ends of foil to seal.
Cooking oil	● In a covered grill arrange preheated coals around a drip pan; test for *medium* heat above pan. Place the stuffed bird, breast side up, on the grill rack over the drip pan but *not* over coals. Brush bird with cooking oil. Insert meat thermometer in the center of the inside thigh muscle, not touching bone. Lower grill hood. Grill for 1¼ to 1½ hours (about 2 hours for capon) or till meat thermometer registers 185°, brushing bird with oil every 30 minutes.
	● Place foil packet of stuffing on grill rack with bird during the last 25 to 30 minutes of grilling to heat through. Makes 6 to 8 servings.

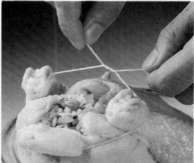

To close the body cavity, wrap a piece of cord around the tail and two legs. Then pull the cord together and tie securely.

To make the bird more compact during grilling, place the bird on its back. Twist the tips of the wings under the back of the bird.

Keg o' Chili

1 pound ground raw turkey
1 medium onion, chopped
2 15-ounce cans chili beans in chili gravy
1 12-ounce can beer
1 7½-ounce can tomatoes, cut up
½ cup chili sauce
1 teaspoon chili powder
¼ teaspoon garlic salt
¼ teaspoon crushed red pepper

● In a large saucepan or Dutch oven cook and stir ground turkey and onion till turkey is no longer pink and onion is tender. Stir in *undrained* beans, beer, *undrained* tomatoes, chili sauce, chili powder, garlic salt, and red pepper.

You'll be a dine-o-mite success when you serve up this chili at your next tailgate party or family dinner. But if feeding a small army isn't for you, freeze the chili in 2-cup (1-serving) portions and use it as ammunition the next time you're caught off guard at mealtime.

Shredded cheddar cheese (optional)
Chopped green pepper (optional)

● Bring to boiling. Reduce the heat. Cook over medium-low heat for 15 to 20 minutes or till heated through, stirring occasionally. Top each serving with cheese and green pepper, if desired. Makes 4 or 5 servings.

Mumbo Gumbo

¾ cup long grain rice
1 12-ounce can spicy vegetable juice cocktail
1 12-ounce can whole kernel corn with sweet peppers
1 10-ounce package frozen cut okra
1 7½-ounce can tomatoes, cut up
1 tablespoon dried minced onion
1 teaspoon instant chicken bouillon granules
1 teaspoon Worcestershire sauce
½ teaspoon dried thyme, crushed
¼ teaspoon garlic powder
¼ teaspoon bottled hot pepper sauce

● Cook rice according to package directions. Meanwhile, in a large saucepan stir together the vegetable juice cocktail, *undrained* corn, okra, *undrained* tomatoes, onion, bouillon granules, Worcestershire sauce, thyme, garlic powder, and hot pepper sauce. Cook, covered, over medium-low heat for 10 to 12 minutes or till okra is crisp-tender, stirring occasionally.

Although traditional gumbos are thickened with filé powder, we've used the thickening power of okra to save you time.

2½ cups cubed cooked chicken

● Stir in chicken. Cook for 5 to 7 minutes more or till heated through. Serve over the hot cooked rice. Makes 4 or 5 servings.

Broccoli-Chicken Soup

2 cups water
2 tablespoons butter *or* margarine
1 10-ounce package frozen chopped broccoli
1 4¾-ounce package noodles and cheese sauce
½ teaspoon dry mustard

● In a large saucepan bring water and butter or margarine to boiling. Add broccoli, noodles and sauce, and mustard. Return to boiling. Continue boiling, uncovered, over medium heat about 7 minutes or till broccoli is crisp-tender, stirring occasionally.

Bits of broccoli, noodles, chicken, and a hint of mustard make this creamy soup a "souper" supper.

2 cups milk
1½ cups cut-up cooked chicken *or* two 5-ounce cans chunk-style chicken, drained
1½ cups shredded American cheese (6 ounces)

● Stir in milk, chicken, and cheese. Cook and stir over medium-high heat for 3 to 5 minutes or till cheese is melted and mixture is heated through. Serves 6.

Easy Chicken-Noodle Soup

2 14½-ounce cans chicken broth
2 cups cut-up cooked chicken *or* two 5-ounce cans chunk-style chicken, drained and flaked
1 10-ounce package frozen peas and carrots
1 tablespoon dried minced onion
½ teaspoon dried thyme, crushed
Dash pepper

● In a large saucepan stir together chicken broth, chicken, frozen peas and carrots, dried minced onion, dried thyme, and pepper. Bring to boiling.

A mom's defense against cold, blustery days—galoshes, mittens, mufflers, and a hot bowl of this chicken soup.

1 cup fine noodles

● Stir in uncooked noodles. Reduce heat. Cover and simmer about 10 minutes or till noodles are tender. Ladle soup into bowls. Makes 4 or 5 servings.

Corn and Lima Chowder

2	slices bacon, cut in half
1½	cups water
1	medium potato, peeled and chopped
1	9- or 10-ounce package frozen corn and lima beans (succotash)
1	tablespoon instant chicken bouillon granules
½	teaspoon dried dillweed
⅛	teaspoon pepper

● In a large saucepan cook bacon till crisp. Drain and crumble. Set aside.

In the same saucepan combine water, potato, corn and lima beans, bouillon granules, dillweed, and pepper. Bring to boiling. Reduce the heat. Simmer, covered, for 10 to 12 minutes or till vegetables are crisp-tender.

"Merci beaucoup" to the French peasants who first developed soup as we know and love it today. However, give some credit to the royalty. If Louis XIV of France hadn't decided soup was food fit for the aristocracy, its fame never would have spread so far.

1½	cups milk
3	tablespoons all-purpose flour
1½	cups cubed cooked chicken *or* turkey
3	green onions, sliced (¼ cup)

● Stir *1 cup* of the milk into saucepan. Stir remaining milk into flour. Stir flour mixture into saucepan. Cook and stir till thickened and bubbly. Cook and stir for 1 minute more. Stir in chicken or turkey and green onions. Heat through. Top each serving with some of the crumbled bacon. Makes 4 servings.

Microwave reheating directions: To reheat 1 serving of soup, micro-cook it in a microwave-safe container, loosely covered with waxed paper, on 100% power (high) for 3 to 5 minutes or till heated through, stirring once.

Curried Chowder

1	medium apple, cored and chopped (1¼ cups)
2	stalks celery, sliced (1 cup)
1	to 1½ teaspoons curry powder
3	tablespoons butter *or* margarine
3	tablespoons all-purpose flour
1⅔	cups chicken broth
1½	cups milk

● In a medium saucepan cook the apple, celery, and curry powder in butter or margarine for 4 to 5 minutes or till apple and celery are crisp-tender. Stir in flour. Add chicken broth and milk all at once. Cook and stir over medium heat till mixture is thickened and bubbly.

Cooking the curry powder in butter helps take the edge off the spice, leaving only a deliciously well-rounded flavor.

1½	cups cubed cooked chicken
½	cup raisins
¼	chopped peanuts

● Stir in chicken and raisins. Cook and stir over medium heat for 5 minutes or till heated through, stirring occasionally. Top each serving with some of the chopped peanuts. Makes 4 servings.

Place a tortilla on top of the hot oil. Using a metal ladle, press the tortilla against the bottom of the pan for 40 to 60 seconds or till tortilla is golden and forms a bowl around the ladle. With tongs, remove tortilla; drain on a rack or on paper towels.

Mexican Chicken Soup in Tortilla Bowls

Cooking oil *or* shortening for deep-fat frying
6 5½-inch corn *or* flour tortillas

2 cups milk
1 10¾-ounce can condensed cream of chicken soup
1 8¾-ounce can whole kernel corn, drained
1 cup chopped tomatoes
1 4-ounce can diced green chili peppers, drained
2 tablespoons minced dried onion
2 cloves garlic, minced
¾ teaspoon dried oregano, crushed
½ teaspoon ground red pepper
1½ cups cubed cooked chicken
1 cup shredded Monterey Jack cheese (4 ounces)
Cherry tomatoes, halved (optional)
Parsley (optional)

● To make tortilla bowls, in a saucepan or deep-fat fryer heat about 2½ inches oil or shortening to 375°. Fry one tortilla at a time, using instructions opposite.

● For soup, in a large saucepan stir together milk and condensed soup; stir in corn, tomatoes, chili peppers, dried onion, garlic, oregano, and ground red pepper. Bring to boiling; reduce heat. Simmer, uncovered, for 5 minutes.

Add chicken and cheese; heat and stir till cheese is melted and chicken is heated through. To serve, place each tortilla bowl in a soup bowl; fill with soup. Garnish with cherry tomatoes and parsley, if desired. Makes 6 servings.

Instead of serving tortilla chips with your soup, serve the soup in a tortilla! Regular corn tortillas become crispy soup bowls when you fry them in hot oil for a minute or less. For softer shells, use flour tortillas. The quick and easy soup makes up for the extra effort you put into making the bowls.

Curried Turkey Burgers

2 tablespoons finely
  chopped onion
1 to 1½ teaspoons curry
  powder
2 teaspoons butter *or*
  margarine
1 teaspoon all-purpose flour
¾ cup plain yogurt

● For curry sauce, in a small saucepan cook onion and curry powder in butter or margarine till onion is tender. Remove from the heat. Stir flour into yogurt, then stir into onion mixture.

1 beaten egg
⅓ cup quick-cooking rolled
  oats
2 tablespoons snipped
  parsley
¼ teaspoon salt
1 pound ground raw turkey

● In a mixing bowl combine egg and *2 tablespoons* curry sauce. Stir in rolled oats, parsley, and salt. Add ground turkey and mix well. Shape turkey mixture into four ¾-inch-thick patties.

Lightly grease an unheated rack in a broiler pan. Place patties on rack. Broil 3 to 4 inches from the heat about 14 minutes or till well done, turning once. *Or,* brush cold grill rack with cooking oil. Grill patties, on an uncovered grill, directly over *medium-hot* coals for 12 to 15 minutes or till well done, turning once.

2 tablespoons finely
  chopped chutney
4 hamburger buns, split and
  toasted

● Meanwhile, stir chutney into remaining curry sauce. Cook and stir just till heated through (*do not boil*).

Serve burgers on buns with sauce. Makes 4 servings.

Here's our favorite blend for homemade curry powder:

In a blender container place 4½ teaspoons ground *coriander,* 2 teaspoons ground *turmeric,* 1¼ teaspoons *cumin seed,* ½ to 1 teaspoon whole *black pepper,* ½ to 1 teaspoon crushed *red pepper,* ½ teaspoon whole *cardamom seed* (without pods), ½ inch stick *cinnamon,* ¼ teaspoon whole *cloves,* and ¼ teaspoon ground *ginger.* Cover and grind for 1 to 2 minutes or till mixture is a fine powder. Store the spice mixture in an airtight container in a cool, dry place. Makes about ¼ cup.

Attention Microwave Owners

Recipes with microwave directions were tested in countertop microwave ovens that have 600 to 700 watts of cooking power. Cooking times are approximate since microwave ovens vary by manufacturer.

Turkey-Veggie Pitas

¼ cup mayonnaise *or* salad
　　dressing
2 tablespoons chutney
¼ to ½ teaspoon curry
　　powder
⅛ teaspoon pepper

● For dressing, in a small mixing bowl stir together mayonnaise or salad dressing, chutney, curry, and pepper.

Sandwiches are a natural stage for demonstrating the versatility of turkey. Here it's starring with avocado, cheese, tomato, sprouts, and chutney-curry dressing, presented in a pita bread half.

1 small avocado, seeded,
　　peeled, and sliced
1 tablespoon lemon juice
2 large pita bread rounds,
　　halved
4 thin slices provolone *or*
　　Swiss cheese (4 ounces)
5 ounces thinly sliced
　　smoked turkey breast
　　portion
1 medium tomato, sliced
1 cup fresh alfalfa sprouts

● Toss avocado slices with lemon juice to prevent browning. For *each* sandwich spread inside of pita half with some of the dressing. Place *1* cheese slice in each pita half. Add ¼ of the turkey slices, tomato slices, and alfalfa sprouts. Top with ¼ of the avocado slices and some of the remaining dressing. Serve immediately. Makes 4 servings.

You'll find that two 2½-ounce packages of very thinly sliced turkey or chicken make a great substitute for the sliced turkey breast portion.

Zucchini-Chicken Salad Sandwiches

2 5-ounce cans chunk-
　　style chicken
¼ cup mayonnaise *or* salad
　　dressing
1 tablespoon horseradish
　　mustard
¼ teaspoon onion powder
⅛ teaspoon pepper
¾ cup shredded zucchini
¼ cup sliced celery

● Drain chicken. Cut up large pieces. In a mixing bowl combine mayonnaise or salad dressing, horseradish mustard, onion powder, and pepper. Mix well. Stir in chicken, zucchini, and celery.

Now here's an original way to use up that extra zucchini that always seems to find its way into refrigerators. The horseradish mustard gives this splendid spin-off of the routine chicken salad sandwich just the gusto it needs.

8 slices rye *or* whole wheat
　　bread
4 lettuce leaves

● Toast bread, if desired. For *each* sandwich, place ¼ of the chicken mixture on *1* slice of bread. Top with a lettuce leaf and another slice of bread. Serves 4.

Chicken and Apple Croissants

1 **5-ounce can chunk-style chicken, drained** ¼ **cup unsalted peanuts, chopped** ¼ **cup raisins**	● In a small mixing bowl stir together chicken, peanuts, and raisins. Cover chicken mixture and place in the freezer for 15 minutes.
⅓ **cup mayonnaise _or_ salad dressing** 2 **teaspoons milk**	● For dressing, in a small mixing bowl stir together mayonnaise or salad dressing and milk. Cover and place in the freezer for 15 minutes.
1 **small apple, cored and chopped** **Lettuce leaves** 2 **croissants, halved horizontally**	● Add apple to chicken mixture. Spoon dressing atop. Toss lightly to coat. Serve chicken mixture in lettuce-lined croissants. Makes 2 servings.

Crazy about curry? Then stir 1 teaspoon _curry powder_ into the dressing. It'll add a spicy kick.

Dressed-Up BLTs

8 **slices bacon** 2 **whole large skinned and boned chicken breasts, halved lengthwise**	● In a 10-inch skillet cook bacon over medium heat till crisp. Drain, reserving _2 tablespoons_ of the drippings in the skillet. Set bacon aside. Meanwhile, place _each_ chicken breast half, boned side up, between 2 pieces of clear plastic wrap. Working from the center to the edges, pound the chicken lightly with the fine-toothed or flat side of a meat mallet to ¼-inch thickness.
	● Cook chicken pieces in reserved bacon drippings over medium heat for 2 to 3 minutes or till lightly browned. Turn and cook for 2 to 3 minutes more or till chicken is no longer pink.
¼ **cup mayonnaise _or_ salad dressing** 1 **tablespoon catsup** ½ **teaspoon Worcestershire sauce** ¼ **teaspoon prepared horseradish** 4 **individual French rolls, split and toasted** 1 **medium tomato, thinly sliced** **Lettuce leaves**	● Meanwhile, in a small mixing bowl stir together mayonnaise or salad dressing, catsup, Worcestershire sauce, and horseradish. Spread roll halves with some of the mayonnaise mixture. For sandwiches, top each roll bottom with lettuce and a piece of chicken. Layer with _2 pieces_ of bacon, some of the tomato, and more lettuce. Top with the roll top, spread side down. Serves 4.

Dare to deck out your next sandwich in style. Try our dressed-up BLT. We've added a sautéed chicken breast fillet and a zippy sauce. Presented on a toasted French roll, it's definitely a chic sandwich!

Garden Delight Sandwich

2 hard-cooked eggs
⅓ cup mayonnaise *or* salad dressing
2 to 3 teaspoons prepared horseradish
1 teaspoon dried dillweed
6 radishes, chopped (⅓ cup)

● Peel and slice the hard-cooked eggs. Set aside. Meanwhile, in a small bowl stir together mayonnaise or salad dressing, horseradish, and dillweed. Stir in chopped radishes.

Use extra-hot horseradish to put more zip into the sandwich.

4 slices pumpernickel bread
4 ounces very thinly sliced chicken *or* turkey
½ small cucumber, thinly sliced

● For *each* sandwich, spread *half* of the mayonnaise mixture on *2* bread slices. Layer spread side of *1* slice with *half* of the chicken or turkey, egg, and cucumber slices. Top with the remaining bread slice, spread side down. Serves 2.

Pineapple-Cheese Rolls

½ of an 8-ounce container soft-style cream cheese with pineapple
2 tablespoons milk
1 cup cubed cooked chicken *or* turkey, *or* one 5½-ounce can chunk-style chicken, drained and broken up
1 4-ounce package shredded cheddar cheese (1 cup)
1 small carrot, shredded
¼ cup toasted pecans *or* almonds, chopped (optional)
Dash ground nutmeg

● In a medium mixing bowl stir together cream cheese and milk. Stir in chicken or turkey; cheddar cheese; carrot; nuts, if desired; and nutmeg. Place in the freezer for 10 to 15 minutes to chill.

Because this sandwich filling is chock-full of goodies, it is fairly stiff. We suggest you serve it on kaiser rolls or a firm-textured bread.

3 kaiser rolls
3 lettuce leaves

● Cut rolls in half horizontally. For *each* sandwich, spread ⅓ of the chicken mixture on the roll bottom. Top with a lettuce leaf and roll top. Serves 3.

Turkey Reuben

1 tablespoon mayonnaise *or* salad dressing
2 slices rye bread
2 ounces thinly sliced cooked turkey breast
¼ cup sauerkraut, well drained
1½ ounces sliced Monterey Jack cheese

● Spread mayonnaise or salad dressing on both slices of bread. Place sliced turkey on 1 bread slice. Top with sauerkraut. Place sliced cheese on sauerkraut, then top with remaining slice of bread. Makes 1 serving.

Pick up cooked turkey breast at either a delicatessen or your grocer's meat case.

Fruity Chicken Sandwiches

¼ cup plain yogurt
1 tablespoon Dijon-style mustard
   Dash ground allspice
1 8¼-ounce can crushed pineapple, well drained, *or* 1 small tart apple, chopped
1 5-ounce can chunk-style chicken, drained and chopped
¼ cup raisins *or* chopped walnuts

● In a medium mixing bowl stir together yogurt, mustard, and allspice. Stir in pineapple or apple, chicken, and raisins or walnuts. Cover and chill till serving.

You've got several delicious possibilities. Combine the chicken mixture with pineapple or apples and with raisins or walnuts. Or invent your own nutty fruit combo.

8 slices whole wheat bread
   Lettuce leaves

● Spread chicken mixture on *4* of the bread slices. Top with lettuce leaves and remaining bread slices. Makes 4 servings.

Spicy Nectar-Fruit Salad

¼ cup dairy sour cream
2 tablespoons salad oil
2 tablespoons peach *or* apricot nectar
2 teaspoons honey
⅛ teaspoon ground nutmeg

● For dressing, in a small mixer bowl using an electric mixer or rotary beater beat together sour cream, oil, nectar, honey, and nutmeg. Cover and chill in the freezer for 10 minutes.

Need to save time? Try this: Use iceberg lettuce instead of the spinach and shred it with a sharp knife.

½ pound spinach, torn
2 2½-ounce packages very thinly sliced chicken *or* turkey, cut into thin strips
1 cup seedless grapes
1 cup cubed cantaloupe
1 cup sliced strawberries
1 stalk celery, bias sliced
¼ cup sunflower nuts

● Meanwhile, in a large bowl combine spinach, chicken or turkey, grapes, cantaloupe, strawberries, and celery. Transfer to 4 individual plates. Pour dressing over each serving. Sprinkle sunflower nuts atop. Makes 4 servings.

Greek Chicken Salad

1 cup loose-pack frozen green beans
2 cups cubed cooked chicken
1 medium cucumber, seeded and chopped
1 cup crumbled feta cheese
1 cup sliced fresh mushrooms
½ cup sliced pitted ripe olives

● In a medium saucepan cook green beans in a small amount of boiling water for 5 to 6 minutes or till beans are crisp-tender. Drain. Rinse with cold water. Let stand covered with cold water.

Meanwhile, in a large mixing bowl combine chicken, cucumber, feta cheese, mushrooms, and olives. Set the chicken mixture in the freezer while preparing the dressing.

Insomnia, bad breath, dandruff, wrinkles, and thinning hair—yogurt cures them all, or so it was once believed. Although yogurt can't really do all this, it can give foods a light tangy taste, and your diet a good helping of many vitamins and minerals.

½ cup mayonnaise *or* salad dressing
¼ cup plain yogurt
¼ teaspoon garlic powder
¼ teaspoon pepper
Lettuce leaves

● For dressing, in a small mixing bowl combine mayonnaise or salad dressing, yogurt, garlic powder, and pepper.

Drain green beans and add to chicken mixture. Pour dressing over chicken mixture. Toss to coat. Serve on lettuce leaves. Makes 4 servings.

Bulgur Chicken Salad

¾ cup bulgur
1½ cups boiling water

● Place bulgur in a bowl. Pour boiling water over bulgur. Let stand for 20 minutes. Drain well.

⅓ cup olive *or* salad oil
⅓ cup lemon juice
1 teaspoon dried mint, crushed
½ teaspoon lemon pepper
¼ teaspoon garlic salt

● Meanwhile, for dressing, in a screw-top jar combine the olive or salad oil, lemon juice, mint, lemon pepper, and garlic salt. Shake to mix well.

2 cups cubed cooked chicken
2 medium tomatoes, peeled, seeded, and chopped
1 small cucumber, seeded and chopped
¾ cup snipped parsley

● In a large mixing bowl combine the drained bulgur, chicken, tomato, cucumber, and parsley. Toss to mix well.

½ cup chopped pecans
Lettuce leaves

● Shake dressing well. Pour over chicken mixture. Toss gently to coat. Place chicken mixture in freezer for 10 minutes to chill. (Keeps up to 2 days in the refrigerator.) Stir in pecans just before serving. Serve the salad on lettuce leaves. Makes 4 servings.

It's not a mirage! By softening the bulgur in boiling water, we have eliminated the need to marinate this traditional Middle Eastern salad overnight. Now you can relish it right away.

Sesame Chicken Salad

3	tablespoons sesame seeds	● In a medium skillet cook sesame seeds over medium heat about 5 minutes or till toasted, stirring occasionally.
1	6-ounce package frozen pea pods	Meanwhile, place pea pods in a colander. Run colander under cool water till thawed. Drain well.

1	8-ounce can pineapple chunks	● Drain pineapple chunks, reserving *1 tablespoon* of the juice. Set aside.
½	of a small head lettuce, shredded, *or* 4 cups torn mixed greens	In a large bowl combine the pineapple chunks, lettuce or mixed greens, chicken, celery, water chestnuts, pea pods, and sesame seeds. Toss to mix well.
2	cups cubed cooked chicken	
1	stalk celery, chopped	
½	of an 8-ounce can sliced water chestnuts, drained	

¼	cup cooking oil	● In a screw-top jar combine the reserved pineapple juice, cooking oil, honey, soy sauce, mustard, and sesame oil. Shake well. Pour over chicken mixture. Toss to coat well. Serves 4.
1	tablespoon honey	
1	tablespoon soy sauce	
2	teaspoons coarse-grain brown mustard	
½	teaspoon sesame oil	

Try a chicken salad that brings the aura of the Far East to your table. It's versatile and refreshing, not just another salad.

The Mango Tango Salad

1	15-ounce can mango slices	● Place the can of mangoes in the freezer. Meanwhile, in a large mixing bowl toss together chicken or turkey, grapes, and almonds. Set aside.
2	cups cubed cooked chicken *or* turkey	
1½	cups seedless red grapes	
1	2½-ounce package sliced almonds, toasted	

¼	cup lemon yogurt	● In a small mixing bowl stir together yogurt, mayonnaise or salad dressing, dillweed, salt, and pepper. Fold into the chicken mixture. Drain and halve mango slices. Gently fold into the chicken mixture. Serve on lettuce leaves. Garnish with kiwi fruit, if desired. Serves 4.
¼	cup mayonnaise *or* salad dressing	
¾	teaspoon dried dillweed	
⅛	teaspoon salt	
⅛	teaspoon pepper	
	Lettuce leaves	
1	kiwi fruit, peeled and sliced (optional)	

Substitute fresh mango when it's in season from May to August. Look for mangoes that are smooth and firm, then let them ripen at room temperature till they soften. The juicy fruit reminds many people of a cross between pineapple and apricot.

Chicken-Vegetable Platter

2 hard-cooked eggs **Sesame-Herb Dressing**	● Peel eggs and cut into quarters. Prepare Sesame-Herb Dressing.
1½ cups cubed cooked chicken **2 cups cauliflower flowerets** *and/or* **thinly sliced cucumber** **1 small tomato, cut into wedges** **1 small carrot, thinly sliced**	● Place chicken in a small bowl. Pour dressing over chicken. Chill in the refrigerator for 15 minutes. Transfer chicken to a serving platter with a slotted spoon, reserving dressing. Arrange the chicken, vegetables, and eggs in groups on the serving platter. Pass reserved dressing. Makes 4 servings.

Sesame-Herb Dressing: In a screwtop jar combine ¼ cup *cooking oil;* 3 tablespoons dry white *wine* or *vinegar;* 2 tablespoons *lemon juice;* 1 tablespoon *sugar;* 1 teaspoon dried *basil,* crushed; ½ teaspoon *salt;* ½ teaspoon *sesame seed;* ¼ teaspoon dried *rosemary,* crushed; and several dashes bottled *hot pepper sauce.* Stir in ½ to 1 teaspoon *sesame oil,* if desired. Cover and shake well.

If you have a little extra time, arrange individual salads on lettuce-lined plates for a bit more personal touch.

Index